2/2/

ORCA
FOOTPRINTS

Nature Out of Balance

HOW INVASIVE SPECIES ARE CHANGING THE PLANET

MERRIE-ELLEN WILCOX

ORCA BOOK PUBLISHERS

Published in Canada and the United States
in 2021 by Orca Book Publishers.
orcabook.com

Library and Archives Canada Cataloguing in Publication

Title: Nature out of balance : how invasive species are
changing the planet / Merrie-Ellen Wilcox.
Names: Wilcox, Merrie-Ellen, author.
Series: Orca footprints.
Description: Series statement: Orca footprints |
Includes bibliographical references and index.
Identifiers: Canadiana (print) 20200271687 |
Canadiana (ebook) 20200271695 | ISBN 9781459823952 (hardcover) |
ISBN 9781459823969 (PDF) | ISBN 9781459823976 (EPUB)
Subjects: LCSH: Introduced organisms—Juvenile literature. |
LCSH: Biological invasions—Juvenile literature.
Classification: LCC QH353 .W54 2021 | DDC j578.6/2—dc23

Library of Congress Control Number: 2020939276

Summary: Part of the nonfiction Orca Footprints series for
middle readers, illustrated with color photographs. Find out about
the global problem of invasive species, the good and the bad,
and what you can do to support the ecosystems around you.

Orca Book Publishers is committed to reducing the consumption
of nonrenewable resources in the making of our books. We make
every effort to use materials that support a sustainable future.

Orca Book Publishers gratefully acknowledges the support for
its publishing programs provided by the following agencies:
the Government of Canada, the Canada Council for the
Arts and the Province of British Columbia through the
BC Arts Council and the Book Publishing Tax Credit.

Front cover images by ygluzberg/Getty Images
and FatCamera/Getty Images
Back cover images by Chudakov/Dreamstime.com, Stan Tekiela
Author/Naturalist/Wildlife Photographer/Getty Images
and CHUTTERSNAP/Unsplash.com
Design by Teresa Bubela
Layout by Dahlia Yuen
Edited by Kirstie Hudson

Printed and bound in China.

24 23 22 21 • 1 2 3 4

*Nootka lupine, native to British Columbia and Alaska, was
introduced in Iceland in 1945 to improve the soil. Now it
is changing Iceland's landscape.* KOTENKO_A/GETTY IMAGES

For Claire and Julian, who never stop teaching and inspiring me.

Contents

CHAPTER ONE
HERE, THERE
AND EVERYWHERE

CHAPTER TWO
WORLDS WITHIN WORLDS

CHAPTER THREE
IT'S COMPLICATED!

CHAPTER FOUR
GETTING A GRIP

Introduction

In April, brightly colored wildflowers fill the Garry oak meadows in Uplands Park.
CHRIS JUNCK

The first thing I see in Uplands Park, a natural area near my home in Victoria, British Columbia, is the Garry oak trees, with their huge trunks, crooked branches, rough gray bark and, in summer, leathery, dark green leaves. In spring, the meadows around the trees are a blue blanket of camas flowers, with patches of hot pink shooting stars, delicate fawn lilies and bright yellow spring gold. In the winter months, the oaks sometimes look ghostly in the mist.

Deeper in the park, though, I see things that don't belong. First the bank of Himalayan blackberry. Then the thickets of English hawthorn and Scotch broom. Worst of all, the English ivy, which smothers everything on the ground and climbs up the oaks, weakening and eventually killing them. All these plants were brought by European settlers. Even the animals I see in the park—gray squirrels, rabbits, cats and sometimes rats—came from elsewhere.

Getting English ivy off Garry oaks is hard work and takes many hands. MERRIE-ELLEN WILCOX

The Europeans had other impacts too. The Lekwungen Peoples once used these meadows to cultivate kwetlal (camas), which grows from a bulb that was an important part of the local diet. They used fire to stop other plants from filling in the meadows, so all available soil could be used for the camas. But the settlers stopped the Lekwungen Peoples from using their traditional practices. Today many of the big oaks are surrounded by dense thickets of snowberries and roses. It's considered too dangerous to burn the meadows, because the fire might spread to all the houses that have been built nearby.

There's always more to the story than we think! So let's keep walking to find out more about the plants and animals we call *invasive species*.

Camas bulbs were an important part of the traditional diet of Indigenous Peoples in the Pacific Northwest. STEPHEN D. SHAWLEY COLLECTION/NEZ PERCE NATIONAL HISTORIC PARK

CHAPTER ONE

Here, There and Everywhere

The white fuzz on this little brown bat's face means it has white-nose syndrome. Caused by a fungus that likely came to North America from Europe, white-nose syndrome is killing millions of bats.

PETE PATTAVINA/USFWS/CC BY 2.0

Eco-Fact

A native species is one that occurs naturally in a place, having evolved there over a long period of time without any help from humans.

Depending on where you live, you've probably heard about invasive species that spell Big Trouble. They're in the news. They might be in your school grounds or even your backyard. Experts might have visited your class to tell you about them. And you might even have been part of a group of volunteers helping in the battle against them. You'll see a few of these "invasion all-stars" throughout the pages of this book.

But first…

WHAT *IS* AN INVASIVE SPECIES, ANYWAY?

Any type of *organism*—a living thing, such as a plant, animal, insect, fish, fungus, virus or bacteria—can be an invasive species. It usually doesn't misbehave in its home *habitat*, where it has evolved as a *native species*. But once it has been moved to a new area, where it is a *non-native species*, it begins to spread and become a bully, causing problems for the native species there—and often for humans as well. That's when we call it a *non-native invasive species*.

Although these organisms are blamed for everything from *extinctions* of native species to billions of dollars in damage to crops and to nature, they aren't "bad" in themselves. The real villains are us—humans!—since we moved them to the new place, whether by accident or on purpose.

MOVERS AND SHAKERS

Species can travel naturally, sometimes thousands of miles, to new regions and even to different continents. In fact, these "invasions" are an essential part of the history of life on Planet Earth. If the first plants hadn't invaded land from the ancient ocean about 500 million years ago, Earth certainly wouldn't be the amazing place it is now! And if species of all kinds hadn't traveled when the ice sheets melted after the Ice Age, things would look very different from the way they do today. Every species must have been "invasive" at some point or it wouldn't have continued to exist.

Very small organisms, like bacteria, can be carried huge distances—across oceans and continents—by wind and air currents. Larger organisms expand their *ranges* (the areas in which they occur naturally) by following the food and other conditions that they need.

But humans have also been moving species around— by accident since they first left Africa more than 100,000 years ago, and on purpose since they became farmers more than 10,000 years ago. In fact, most of the species that have spread to new places in the last several centuries were moved there by us. We're the all-star *vector* for non-native species.

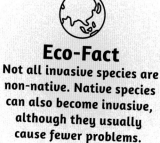

Eco-Fact
Not all invasive species are non-native. Native species can also become invasive, although they usually cause fewer problems.

Eco-Fact
Weed is simply a label we give to plants that grow where we don't want them—usually in our gardens and in farmers' fields. A weed typically grows or spreads rapidly, and it can be a native species or a non-native species.

This modern liverwort's ancestors were likely among the first land plants. They managed to change the earth's climate, alter its soils and allow other life to evolve. ED RESCHKE/GETTY IMAGES

Ballast water emptied from ships moves species around the world every day.
PHIL AUGUSTAVO/GETTY IMAGES

Debris from the 2011 Japanese earthquake and tsunami, like this boat that washed up on an Oregon beach two years later, carried hundreds of species to North America.
STEVEN RUMRILL, SHELLFISH PROGRAM LEADER/
OREGON DEPARTMENT OF FISH AND WILDLIFE

ACCIDENTAL HITCHHIKERS

We move species accidentally in lots of different ways. For example, early humans probably had seeds from plants in their hair and clothes or on their tools, dropping them as they traveled to new regions.

But the main source of accidental movement of species today is international trade. The **globalization** of our economies and culture has also caused the globalization of many species. Insects can hitchhike on the fruits and vegetables, grain and wood that we get from and send all over the world. Snails, slugs and bugs can also be hidden on plants traveling from faraway places to our gardens. Reptiles and amphibians can travel to new homes in cargo containers. Scientists estimate that more than 10,000 species a day are being carried in ships' **ballast water** (taken onboard in one place to balance the ship and its load and then dumped in another part of the world when it unloads), including fish, shellfish, algae, fungi, viruses and bacteria. The more stuff we buy and sell, the more nonnative species move around.

Even the stuff we throw away, including all the plastic that ends up in the oceans, carries countless creatures from one continent to another. Scientists say that our trash could be responsible for a new wave of invasive species on our coasts. Mussels, barnacles and sea squirts can survive for years attached to plastic and eventually wash up on distant shores, ready to take up residence.

The massive 2011 earthquake and tsunami in Japan pulled five million tons of debris into the Pacific Ocean. Currents and storms carried some of it all the way to the west coast of North America. Everything from small pieces of plastic to docks and entire fishing boats served as rafts for a mass migration of marine creatures. Researchers have found almost 300 species that survived the trip.

Lake
St. Clair

Legend:
- non-contaminated provinces/states
- status unknown provinces/states
- contaminated provinces/states

This map shows how far zebra mussels (right), and the closely related quagga mussel, have spread since they were first identified in Lake St. Clair in the mid-1980s.

MAP COURTESY OF CENTRAL KOOTENAY INVASIVE SPECIES SOCIETY/
DATA COURTESY OF THE US GEOLOGICAL SOCIETY/FREEVECTORMAPS.COM

BOB NICHOLS/US DEPARTMENT OF AGRICULTURE   20120106-OC-AMW-0189

INVASIVE ALL-STARS:
Zebra Mussels

In the mid-1980s a European ship released some zebra mussels, likely from its ballast water, into Lake St. Clair, a small lake between Ontario and Michigan that connects Lakes Huron and Erie. Originally from the Caspian Sea in Asia, the mussels spread rapidly throughout the Great Lakes and the waterways linked to them.

Zebra mussels attach to hard surfaces in huge numbers, tens of thousands of them to a square yard (square meter). They clog pipes, screens and other equipment, costing businesses and communities money. They cling to native mussels and clams, smothering them. And when they filter water through their bodies, toxins get concentrated in them, which can then harm the birds and other wildlife that eat them.

IT SEEMED LIKE A GOOD IDEA AT THE TIME...

Of course, humans move all kinds of plants and animals around on purpose as well. Especially in the last few centuries, we've moved thousands of species to new regions, including plants for food crops, mammals for livestock and hunting, birds for pleasure, shellfish for food, fish for sportfishing and aquariums, and reptiles and amphibians for the pet trade. We've always meant well, but the results haven't always been good.

Starting in the late 1400s, for example, when Europeans began to establish colonies in the Americas, India and parts of southeast Asia, they didn't just bring things like corn, potatoes and tobacco home with them. They also took their favorite plants and animals with them wherever they went.

In the mid-1800s French and British naturalists formed ***acclimatization societies*** aimed at getting exotic plants and animals from their colonies to survive in their own countries. European newcomers to North America, New Zealand and Australia then did the reverse, bringing favorite species from Europe to their new homes, often because they were homesick and thought these new lands were somehow less beautiful. Most of the transplants didn't survive, but some of those that did became ecological and economic disasters, like house sparrows and European starlings in North America and rabbits and foxes in Australia.

Thomas Jefferson, third president of the United States and principal author of the Declaration of Independence, believed "the greatest service which can be rendered any country is to add a useful plant to its culture." As a diplomat in France, he sent home seeds of grasses, fruits and vegetables.
WHITE HOUSE COLLECTION/WHITE HOUSE HISTORICAL ASSOCIATION

In the 19th century, a French acclimatization society made this chart showing 75 animals, birds, fish and plants that should be brought to France.
PERROT AND OUDART, 1854.
COURTESY OF GEOGRAPHICUS RARE ANTIQUE MAPS (GEOGRAPHICUS.COM)

These are just a few of North America's 200 million starlings, flying together in what is known as a murmuration.
RICHARD EVANS/SHUTTERSTOCK.COM

INVASIVE ALL-STARS: *Starlings*

In the late 1800s Eugene Schieffelin had a crazy idea—to bring all the birds that William Shakespeare ever mentioned in his plays and poetry to New York's Central Park. This resulted in several poor chaffinches, nightingales and skylarks starving or freezing to death. But 80 starlings from England, released in the park in 1890, had a different fate. They not only survived but thrived, and not just in New York but in towns, cities and agricultural areas across North America.

All of this continent's 200 million European starlings are descendants of those first 80 birds released to a new world over a century ago. Most people, especially farmers, wouldn't thank Mr. Schieffelin, though. Flocks of starlings eat seeds just planted in fields and tear up young plants. They steal and contaminate food and water intended for cows, chickens and other livestock. They carry diseases that can spread to livestock and people. And they compete with native birds for nesting sites and food, sometimes causing species to decline.

NOT QUITE ACCORDING TO PLAN

People have been using certain species to control other species for thousands of years. The first recorded use of a **biological control** was in ancient Egypt, 4,000 years ago, when people were told that cats were useful in controlling rodents. Today we control pests like aphids by introducing large numbers of their natural enemies, such as ladybugs. Sometimes, if there is no natural **predator** available, one is brought in from somewhere else.

Ladybugs eat lots of aphids. (But it turns out these harlequin ladybirds from Asia also eat native ladybugs in North America and Europe.)
FIREFLYPHOTO/DREAMSTIME.COM

One of the best examples of a successful biological control was the introduction of a non-native moth in the 1920s to control the non-native prickly pear cactus, which had covered 59 million acres (24 million hectares) of northeastern Australia. In just a decade, large amounts of farmland had been cleared of prickly pear.

But occasionally this approach has backfired. The introduced species starts to eat all the wrong things and enjoy its new home so much that it decides to stick around. When the harlequin ladybird was brought from Asia to North America in the 1980s and to Europe in the 1990s to control aphids, it started eating native ladybugs as well and went on to become one of the world's most invasive insect species.

The cactus moth, a native of South America, eliminated invasive prickly pear cactus in Australia. But the moth is now invasive in areas where prickly pear is native.
PEGGY GREB, USDA AGRICULTURAL RESEARCH SERVICE

INVASIVE ALL-STARS: *Cane Toads*

In 1935 native beetles were damaging Australia's sugarcane crops. A giant South American toad was being used to control cane-eating beetles in Hawaii, so government scientists went there and captured a small number of the toads. Back in Australia they bred them and, a few months later, released 2,400 toads in the hope that they would eat the beetles. They didn't.

The toads preferred other local insects and happily began to hop far beyond the cane fields.

Cane toads are *big*. They're 6 inches (15 centimeters) long and can weigh more than 2 pounds (1 kilogram). More importantly, they're poisonous, killing anything that tries to eat them. So not only did the toads kill off any possible predators, including reptiles,

birds and mammals, but their numbers and their range also grew. Today there are 1.5 billion cane toads spread over almost 400,000 square miles (1 million square kilometers) of the continent. And they're still moving about 30 miles (50 kilometers) westward each year, causing the decline of many native species as they go.

Cane toads are the world's largest toad. When they are threatened, glands in their skin release a poison that can kill animals that touch the toads, especially dogs.
ISONPHOTO/DREAMSTIME.COM

INVADER NUMBER ONE

Of course, there's another thing about humans in this story, besides our habit of moving plants, animals, insects and other organisms around the world. With the explosive growth in our numbers, and the destructive ways in which parts of our population have chosen to treat our planet, we're actually the most invasive species of all!

Scientists estimate that the world's human population 10,000 years ago was less than 2.5 million. By the beginning of the **Common Era**, it had increased to just under 200 million, growing gradually until about 1400 CE, when it began to explode. Today there are 7.7 billion of us—in almost every corner of every continent except Antarctica—and our numbers are still growing.

Especially since about 1750, with the beginning of the **Industrial Revolution** and the rise of **capitalism**, some of us have consumed huge amounts of resources. We have polluted our environment. We've changed **ecosystems** in countless ways. And sometimes we've driven other species to extinction. So when we blame other non-native invasive species for misbehaving, we should remember that we're responsible for their behavior—*and* we're one of them.

Eco-Fact
Many scientists agree that we are now living in a new age, called the *Anthropocene* (from *anthropo* for "human" and *cene* for "new"), because humans have altered the planet, its atmosphere and its climate.

The human population has exploded since the Industrial Revolution, leaving no ecosystem on Earth untouched by our activities.
ANTON WATMAN/SHUTTERSTOCK.COM

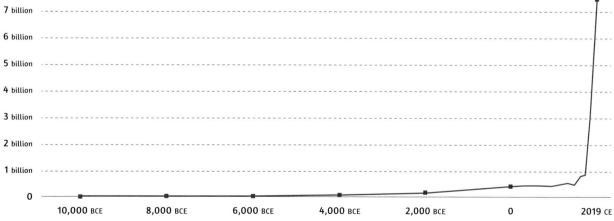

WORLD POPULATION OVER THE LAST 12,000 YEARS

(y-axis: 7 billion, 6 billion, 5 billion, 4 billion, 3 billion, 2 billion, 1 billion, 0)
(x-axis: 10,000 BCE, 8,000 BCE, 6,000 BCE, 4,000 BCE, 2,000 BCE, 0, 2019 CE)

MAX ROSER, HANNAH RITCHIE AND ESTEBAN ORTIZ-OSPINA (UPDATED 2019), "WORLD POPULATION GROWTH," FROM OURWORLDINDATA.ORG/WORLD-POPULATION-GROWTH

CHAPTER TWO

Worlds within Worlds

ALL SYSTEMS GO

A *system* is a group of things that are connected and work together in an organized way. Each part of a system is affected by being in the system, and the system is changed if any part of it is taken away.

Everything we know is part of a system, from the tiniest *cells* that make up every organism—and even the things that make up those cells—to our solar system, the galaxy it is part of and the universe beyond that. And these systems are connected with and nested within each other, affecting each other in infinitely complex ways.

Picture it this way. Each of us is made up of trillions of cells, and each of those cells is not only a system but also belongs to larger systems (like those consisting of our bones and muscles, our organs and our veins and arteries) that all work together to make *us* work. And in turn we're part of many larger systems that we both influence and are influenced by—our families, our communities, our environment and, ultimately, the whole ecosystem that is Planet Earth.

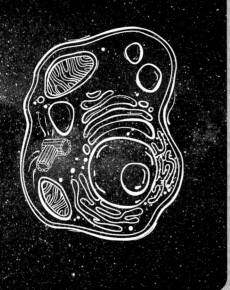

From the smallest cells in our bodies to the Milky Way and beyond, everything is part of a system.
[MILKY WAY] FELIXMITTERMEIER/PIXABAY
[ANIMAL CELL] AGLIA83/DREAMSTIME.COM

All the organisms in this small ecosystem on a log in the forest are connected with each other and with their environment.

KYRYL GORLOV/DREAMSTIME.COM

ALL TOGETHER NOW

An ecosystem is made up of a group of living things—on land, in water and in the air—that are connected in different ways with each other and with the nonliving parts of their environment, such as water, oxygen and sunlight. An ecosystem can be as small as the community of creatures living in a puddle or on a log or as large as the oceans or the boreal forest, which circle the planet. And all of the planet's ecosystems make up the huge system that is Earth.

Each organism in an ecosystem does certain things to get what it needs to survive, such as food, water, shelter and a way to reproduce. Since everything in an ecosystem is connected, what an organism does affects everything else in the system. Removing a species from an ecosystem can affect all the other species. And so can *adding* a new species. Everything is affected, for better or worse.

Even the smallest ecosystems are incredibly complex, having evolved over extremely long periods of time. It's almost impossible to map out all the ways in which organisms interact with each other and the nonliving things in an ecosystem. And with so many organisms interacting, so many processes at work and so many other factors involved, like weather, ecosystems are always adjusting and adapting. And that means they never stand still.

INVASIVE ALL-STARS: *Yellow Crazy Ants*

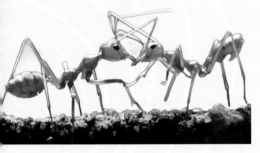

One supercolony contains about 7.5 billion yellow crazy ants.

THEKRIT/SHUTTERSTOCK.COM

Christmas Island is a remote Australian territory in the Indian Ocean. Among the plants and animals people have brought with them—by accident and on purpose—since they settled on the island 120 years ago is the yellow crazy ant. (They're called "crazy" ants because of their frantic movements when they are disturbed.) Good at hitching rides on ships and planes, the ants probably arrived on a ship between 1915 and 1934. For a few decades they didn't do much damage. But since 1989, when their first **supercolony** was found on the island, the yellow crazy ant has been a superpest.

A supercolony contains many interconnected nests with hundreds of queens. The ants eat native animals and insects and compete with them for food. (They also spray formic acid, which can harm much larger animals, including people!) But by working together with another non-native species, a type of sapsucking insect called the yellow lac scale, the ants kill trees, reduce soil health, change the makeup of forests and help other non-native species invade.

The yellow crazy ant has quickly changed large areas of Christmas Island's forest and depleted an important native species, the red land crab. Removing the land crabs has allowed the non-native giant African land snail to spread, causing even more problems. Meanwhile the ant has spread through many of the world's tropical and subtropical regions, including Australia itself.

NEW KIDS ON THE BLOCK

Kudzu was planted for decades in the southern United States before it became "the vine that ate the South."

COURTESY NATIONAL ARCHIVES, PHOTO NO. 83-G-44635

Only a small number of non-native species introduced to ecosystems far from where they came from actually become invasive. Most organisms that are moved from one place to another—whether by natural processes like wind or ocean currents or by people—don't survive. After all, they need exactly the right conditions. In addition to the right food, water and light, they need the right temperatures, mates or pollinators so they can reproduce, and no predators to gobble them up.

But if the conditions in the new place are more or less right for the non-native species, it might begin to settle in. If it's able to reproduce without human help, it becomes *established*. Many non-native species get to this point and don't cause any problems. But if they start to spread and affect the native ecosystem or humans, that's when they become *invasive*.

TAKING OVER

There are other reasons why some non-native species become invasive.

If lots of individual organisms of a species arrive in the new place, whether all at once or again and again over time, they have a much better chance of getting established and starting to spread.

Some ecosystems—especially islands—are more likely than others to be invaded by non-native species. Many islands have species that exist only there and nowhere else in the world, because they've evolved over thousands of years. These species may have small numbers of individual organisms, especially if the island is small. They may have special diets or behaviors that allow them to survive in the harsh conditions that many islands offer, and these can be affected if the conditions change. Island species may also have evolved without any predators, so if a predator suddenly arrives, they have no way to protect themselves, and they can't escape to new areas.

On many islands there are now more non-native species of plants and animals than native ones. Of the more than 700 known animal extinctions in the past 400 years, more than half were on islands. And most of the bird extinctions have been on islands.

Other ecosystems more likely to be invaded by non-native species are those that have been damaged and are no longer working well. Many ecosystems are being affected by rising temperatures, more or less rainfall and larger and more frequent fires caused by *climate change*. Or they might have been damaged by pollution, chemicals such as *pesticides* and fertilizers, forest clear-cutting, hydroelectric dams, urban sprawl and many other impacts of human activity. Introduced into these places, some non-native species thrive on those altered conditions and quickly become invasive.

Ships like these, used by European explorers, traders and colonists, introduced many non-native species to fragile island ecosystems around the world.
WELLCOME COLLECTION. CC BY 4.0

The dodo bird, native to the island of Mauritius, was driven to extinction, likely by rats from European ships.
BUFFON, GEORGES LOUIS LECLERC, COMTE DE. 1799. HISTOIRE NATURELLE : GENERALE ET PARTICULIERE T. 57, PARIS : F. DUFART

Kudzu has completely overtaken this landscape in Mississippi.
CMOULTON/DREAMSTIME.COM

INVASIVE ALL-STARS: *Kudzu*

If you live in the southeastern United States, you probably know kudzu. The climbing vine behaves itself in its native range in Asia. And for the first few decades after it was introduced to North America from Japan in 1876, it provided welcome shade for porches, fed cattle and prevented soil erosion. By 1946 about 3 million acres (1.2 million hectares) had been planted, including 85 million seedlings the US government paid to have planted for erosion control.

Today American kudzu is anything but well behaved. Growing about a foot per day in the summer, it is found in about 227,000 acres (92,000 hectares) of forest and is still spreading by up to 2,500 acres (1,000 hectares) per year. It kills or damages most other plants by smothering them. The only plants that can compete with it are other nasty invaders, like Chinese privet and Japanese honeysuckle. People have called kudzu "the vine that ate the South."

THE STORY OF GUAM AND THE BROWN TREE SNAKE

On the island of Guam, brown tree snakes cause power outages when they slither along hydro lines. USDA/APHIS/CC BY 2.0

The island of Guam is an American territory in the western Pacific Ocean. About 30 miles (almost 50 kilometers) long and 10 miles (16 kilometers) wide, it was an important military base during World War II. In the 1940s, some brown tree snakes hitched a ride to the island—possibly aboard ships or planes moving military equipment from other islands. By the 1960s the snakes had infested half the island. The rest of the island was infested by the 1970s, and by the 1980s there were about 250 snakes per acre (100 per hectare). Today there are an estimated 2 million snakes on the island, more than 10 times the human population.

Three feet (one meter) long, with sharp fangs and bulgy eyes, brown tree snakes eat everything—native birds and animals, livestock, pets. Ten of Guam's bird species went extinct after the snakes' arrival, which in turn affected fruit trees that relied on the birds for spreading their seeds. Several species of native bats and lizards also went extinct. The snakes climb trees, of course, but also buildings and even utility poles, where they slither along the wires looking for bird snacks—and weigh down the lines enough to cause almost daily power outages.

It's easy to blame the snake. But some *ecologists* (scientists who study ecosystems) remind people that Guam's ecosystems had already been severely damaged, first by the clearing of forests to make way for coconut plantations, then by bombing during the war, clearing of land for the military base and all the housing and other development needed to support it, and finally by the spraying of pesticides to rid the island of mosquitos carrying malaria. Many native species were already struggling before the brown tree snake's arrival.

MAKING ECO-MISCHIEF

Since ecosystems are complex, the impacts of non-native invasive species are also complex. Invasive plants can crowd out native species just by their numbers. They can change conditions, such as the amounts of light, water and nutrients available for other species. Invasive animals and fish can eat up all the food that native species need—or eat native species themselves or their eggs and young. Invasive insects can kill entire populations of certain trees and other plants, which affects everything else in the ecosystem.

Especially in small, isolated ecosystems like islands and small lakes, non-native species invasions can help drive native species to extinction. With certain species spreading to larger and more

Eco-Fact
Humans have been changing ecosystems for thousands of years—often in positive ways—by hunting, saving seeds to grow certain plants and tilling the soil. Indigenous Peoples in North America regularly used fire to manage their lands, and over time plants that couldn't survive fire were replaced by plants that needed fire—for example, to release their seeds so they could grow. European settlers stopped practices like these, which then weakened the ecosystems that had come to depend on them.

Water hyacinth, seen here in Siem Reap, Cambodia, is native to South America but has spread around the world. Each plant can double itself in 5 to 15 days.
LARISSA BERGEMANN/DREAMSTIME.COM

First brought to North and South America by Europeans in the 1500s, the smallpox virus eventually killed much of the Indigenous population.
CALLISTA IMAGES/GETTY IMAGES

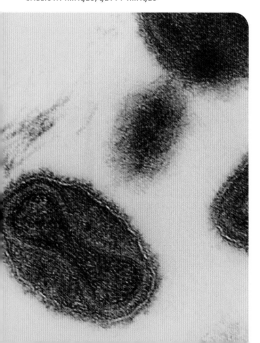

parts of the world, they are making ecosystems around the world less diverse and more like each other.

Non-native invasive species have also been called one of the greatest threats to *biodiversity* on the planet—along with climate change, loss of habitat, pollution and overhunting. Biodiversity is the variety and variability of living things in an ecosystem. More biodiversity means a healthier ecosystem (and planet), able to survive challenges like fire and storms. We all depend on the world's biodiversity.

HARMING HUMANS

Pathogens that cause diseases in humans and other organisms can be invasive too.

Bacteria and viruses that spread to new places can threaten human health directly. A tragic example was smallpox. People in northern Africa, Asia and Europe were exposed to the virus for thousands of years. About a third of the people who caught it died. But when Europeans carried the virus to North and South America, starting in the 1500s, Indigenous Peoples there had never been exposed to it and had no immunity. Some communities lost most of their members, and others were wiped out completely. Some historians believe that 20 million people died—up to 95 percent of the population of the Americas.

Diseases and non-native pests (such as insects) that harm plants and animals also affect us indirectly. Damage to crops and livestock can affect our food supply. Controlling diseases and pests also costs farmers a lot of money. Farmers in poor countries are hardest hit, as they may not be able to afford pesticides or other means of reducing damage. Some non-native plants, such as cheatgrass, which covers millions of acres in western North America, can make regions more prone to wildfires. They burn easily and provide lots of fuel for fires, which can threaten people's health and their property.

We depend on healthy ecosystems in many different ways. They provide us with food, fresh water, medicines, wood and fiber. They regulate climate and purify air and water. Our cultures depend on them. These benefits are called *ecosystem services*, and we couldn't live without them. Because non-native invasive species damage ecosystems, they also affect ecosystem services, which in turn affects *us*.

Fall armyworm can feed on more than 80 crops, but it prefers maize (corn), a staple crop, especially in Africa. The worm threatens the food security of 300 million Africans.
PHILIPPE DEMANDE/DREAMSTIME.COM

INVASIVE ALL-STARS: *Chestnut Blight*

Until 100 years ago, the American chestnut was one of the most important trees in eastern North America. Its seeds provided food for wildlife and people and an income for those who gathered and sold them. Its wood was used for everything from furniture to railroad ties. And the huge, leafy trees were an important part of the landscape.

But in 1904 a fungus was brought to the continent on garden plants from Asia. Dead trees were first spotted at the Bronx Zoo, and in 40 years the chestnut blight had spread throughout the tree's entire range. For the many people who had depended on the chestnut tree for wood and income or even just for its beauty and shade, the impact was large and long-lasting.

Scientists are still trying to develop an American chestnut that is resistant to the blight, in the hope that the tree will once again fill the forests.

Chestnut blight changed the American landscape, killing virtually all the huge, leafy trees.
[LIVING TREE] GAIL WHISTANCE/CC BY-ND
[DEAD TREE] JACK BOUCHER/
US NATIONAL PARK SERVICE

CHAPTER THREE

It's Complicated!

For many problems, big and small, the best solution is prevention. And if you can't prevent a problem, you have to find ways to deal with it. The same goes for non-native invasive species. (Warning: Like the problem itself, the solutions are anything but simple. Managing invasive species is complicated!)

STEMMING THE FLOW

Ecologists around the world are working to better understand what makes non-native species become invasive. The more they understand, the more likely they'll be able to predict which species in which ecosystems will become troublemakers—or at least what their impacts will be. And if ecologists can make accurate predictions, governments can take action and create rules and laws to prevent people from moving problem species.

When scientists figured out that the ballast system in ships carrying goods around the world every day was moving thousands of marine species as well, governments and international organizations created rules about where and when ships could release ballast water. Researchers are also developing ways of

Eco-Fact

Lots of people work together to manage non-native invasive species. Ecologists, biologists and other scientists and researchers might work with *restoration ecologists* (people who work to restore damaged ecosystems) and *conservation managers* (people who work to protect species and habitats), and they often rely on citizen scientists and other volunteers for help.

Giant hogweed, originally from southwest Asia, is spreading throughout North America. The scientists are wearing gloves because the plant's sap is toxic and causes burns. CHUDAKOV/DREAMSTIME.COM

treating ballast water before it's released to ensure that the hitch-hikers won't stick around. Another idea is to build ships with open-ended tubes running their length, with only local water flowing through the tubes as ballast as the ship moves.

Ecologists and governments can also use the ***precautionary principle*** when deciding whether a species should be brought into a country or region—for example, to be used to control an insect or other pest. This means that only species they know for sure will do no harm can be moved. Cane toads wouldn't have been brought to Australia back in the 1930s if scientists had followed the precautionary principle. They didn't know enough about the toads, by today's standards, to be sure that their planned biological control wouldn't cause any problems in Australian ecosystems.

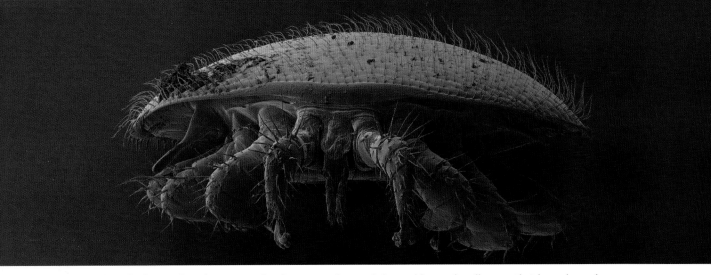

Originally from Indonesia, varroa mites have spread around the world, carrying diseases that harm honeybees. They're not this big, thankfully, but you can see them on bees without a microscope. VERASTUCHELOVA/DREAMSTIME.COM

SOUNDING THE ALARM

With so many species on the move via our ships and planes, even the strictest rules aren't always going to work. Some species are still going to cross our borders, no matter how hard we try to keep them out. The next best strategy is to know right away when something has landed, so that we can take immediate action.

Here's a great example. Australia is one of the only places left in the world where honeybees don't have varroa mites, which carry viruses and diseases that harm the bees. When a colony of sick honeybees was reported on an American ship that had docked in Melbourne in 2018, government scientists quickly destroyed the colony. They then inspected and monitored "sentinel hives" in the port, kept just for attracting mites if they arrive on a ship, as well as gardens within 1.25 miles (2 kilometers) of the port. And so far, Australia is still mite-free.

Detecting a non-native species before it has become invasive isn't always easy, though. Often by the time it's been spotted, it's already too late. Scientists are exploring some high-tech methods of **early detection** that might help. Drones and satellites equipped with special cameras can help them identify newly introduced species before they spread too far. DNA testing is being used as well, especially for small species that are hard to identify.

Eco-Fact
Some scientists worry that *genetically modified organisms (GMOs)*, like those being developed for use as biofuels (plants used as fuels for transportation and industry), might become invasive non-native plants created right here at home. They're often bred from non-native plants *because* they spread easily, grow densely (crowding other things out) and resist pests—all key qualities of invasive plants!

STAMPING THEM OUT

As soon as a non-native species arrives in a new ecosystem, it begins to change the ecosystem. And the longer it stays, the more and the bigger the changes. That means it's really only possible to *eradicate* (get rid of) a non-native species from an ecosystem when it hasn't spread too far and hasn't been there too long.

Plants can sometimes be pulled out with tools and hands. If that's not possible, a biological control might be used, like a beetle or other insect—or even goats. Larger animals such as mice and rats (rodents) can be trapped, shot or poisoned. Fish can sometimes be caught one at a time or trapped in large numbers. Biological controls are sometimes used for insects, often by introducing a predator or disease from their native habitat. People frequently resort to using pesticides (chemicals that kill plants, insects and other organisms). And sometimes all available methods are used together.

Tools, time and energy can sometimes be used to help eradicate invasive plants like English ivy. MERRIE-ELLEN WILCOX

On islands, rats eat seabird eggs, which means the birds can't reproduce. With the birds gone, the whole ecosystem changes.
BERNHARD SCHARINGER/DREAMSTIME.COM

INVASIVE ALL-STARS: *Rats*

Rats are infamous for spreading diseases that affect humans, including plague, which caused the Black Death in Asia, North Africa and Europe starting in the 1300s. But rats are also known as nasty non-native invasive species. For centuries Polynesian and European explorers accidentally took ashore some of the rodents living on their boats and ships. The rats then invaded and, especially on islands, changed ecosystems, driving many native species of birds, reptiles and small mammals to decline or extinction.

People have been working for decades to eradicate rats from islands around the world. It's not easy. Some rat species are important to specific cultures—like the Pacific rat for the Maori—so getting rid of them when they are harming ecosystems can create cultural tensions. Rats are also famously hard to catch.

In one experiment, researchers released a single rat on a small New Zealand island to find out how long it would take to capture it again. It took 10 weeks and nine different methods, including trained dogs, three different kinds of trap and two different types of bait (including peanut butter)!

Although the efforts to rid islands of rats don't always work, they're getting better. In some places, rat poison is being dropped by helicopters and drones, which is faster and less expensive than placing it by hand and can be used on larger islands.

KEEPING A LID ON THEM

Once a non-native species has spread to a larger area or to several areas, it's almost impossible to get rid of it. But it may be possible to control it and its impacts, either by stopping it from spreading farther or by keeping the population below a certain level.

To do this, ecologists bring together their knowledge of the species and the ecosystem and all the technologies and methods available. Then they monitor the results of their efforts so they can adjust them as needed.

Sometimes researchers invent new technologies to deal with specific species. In Hawaii, a special underwater vacuum cleaner is helping remove a thick blanket of invasive algae from coral reefs. Divers used the Super Sucker to remove 40,000 pounds (more than 18,000 kilograms) of algae, covering 6 acres (almost 2.5 hectares) of reef, without damaging the coral or its remaining inhabitants. Then they introduced 99,000 native sea urchins to clean up the remaining green stuff. The algae removed by the super sucker was then given to local farmers to use as fertilizer for their crops. Researchers believe they were able to remove about 85 percent of the algae.

A diver removes invasive algae from coral using a Super Sucker. BRIAN NEILSON/DIVISION OF AQUATIC RESOURCES/STATE OF HAWAII

INVASIVE ALL-STARS: *Asian Carp*

Asian carp were introduced in the southeastern United States in the 1970s to control weeds and pests in fish-farm ponds. Floods released them into nearby creeks and rivers that flowed into the Mississippi River, and they've been spreading northward ever since. Very large and hungry fish—some of them can grow to 3 feet (a meter) in length and weigh as much as 90 pounds (40 kilograms)—they crowd out native species by eating all their food. Some of them can jump up to 10 feet (3 meters) out of the water if they're startled and have seriously injured people in boats.

Scientists and engineers are trying a variety of ways to prevent the carp from spreading into the Great Lakes—from walls and fences to electrical currents and high-pressure blasts of water that make the fish head back to where they were coming from. Governments on both sides of the Great Lakes are monitoring the fish very carefully, as well as trying to educate people about things they shouldn't do, such as dumping water from bait buckets that might contain carp eggs or babies.

29

Eco-Fact

EASIER SAID THAN DONE

One of the biggest challenges for ecologists is that it's hard to predict how a non-native species will act when it lands in a new place. Every ecosystem is a little different, so a non-native species might act differently in each place. Ecologists also have to consider the effects of climate change on the ecosystem and the species—not only today but also in the future, which is full of unknowns.

Using pesticides to deal with invasive species can have its own serious impacts on ecosystems. These chemicals rarely affect just the non-native species—they can harm native species as well. They can build up in the ecosystem or spread out into neighboring ecosystems. For example, raptors that eat poisoned rodents may also end up being poisoned, creating further impacts on the ecosystem. The invasive species can also become resistant, so the chemical no longer works.

And since ecosystems are so complex, ecologists may not be able to predict the effects of their efforts to manage an invasive species. Things can go wrong in a number of other ways too. Removing invasive pigs and goats from Sarigan Island in the

Goats are used around the world to control invasive plants. But left on islands they become invasive themselves, stripping the ecosystem of native vegetation. C. JOSH DONLAN

Kudzu bugs are great at destroying kudzu vine, but they're also good at destroying crops such as soybeans.

Pacific Ocean in order to protect native plants allowed one of the goats' favorite foods, a non-native vine, to go wild. Within two years the vine covered most of the small island.

Sometimes, though, even the nastiest invasive species can take a hit from another one. A Japanese kudzu bug hitched a plane ride to Atlanta, Georgia, in 2009 and is now starting to kill off the monster kudzu vine. (The dying plants smell a bit like grape bubble gum.) The bug is also becoming yet another headache for farmers and homeowners, as it damages crops and infests homes during the winter. (It also lets off an unpleasant smell—*not* like bubble gum—when it's disturbed.)

For these reasons, and some other surprising facts that we'll look at in chapter 4, some scientists and writers are wondering whether we need to start thinking a little differently about non-native invasive species.

CHAPTER FOUR

Getting a Grip

Just as we need to avoid xenophobia in society, we may need to start thinking differently about some non-native species.
JOHNNY SILVERCLOUD/SHUTTERSTOCK.COM

Eco-Fact

Some people argue that we shouldn't use the terms *native* and *non-native* species at all, since species have been changing and on the move in one way or another forever. How long does a species have to be in one place before it's considered "native"?

THINKING DIFFERENTLY

Ecologists have traditionally used military words like *invaders* and *the enemy* for non-native invasive species, and their work is often described as "the war against invasive species." As humans, we do tend to look at things in black and white—as us and them, good and bad, friends and enemies—rather than seeing all the shades of gray in between. That is the root of **xenophobia**, the fear and hatred of strangers or foreigners, and our habit of **othering**, which is seeing or treating people or groups as alien to ourselves.

A growing number of scientists are suggesting that just as we need to avoid this kind of thinking in our societies, we also need to move away from it in ecology. Many non-native species are here to stay, no matter what we call them. It's unlikely we'll get rid of the 750 trillion zebra mussels in the Great Lakes or the 200 million starlings in North America. They're not going back to where they came from. We're facing many other large environmental problems as well, like pollution and climate change, and we have limited time and dollars to deal with them all.

So maybe, in addition to focusing on prevention, we need to "fight" only the most damaging invasive species and the ones we have a realistic chance of "winning" against, and look harder for ways we might benefit from the others.

FINDING THE SILVER LINING

Some non-native invasive species cause big problems for ecosystems and for humans. But many do not. In fact, some can even be helpful.

The impacts of non-native species on native species often lessen over time, as both the native and non-native species adapt and the ecosystem finds a new balance. In Australia, native species that used to try to eat cane toads are learning to eat only the nontoxic parts of the toad or to avoid it altogether!

When a native species has been lost, non-native species can sometimes do their jobs. In parts of Europe, for instance, where a disease wiped out several native crayfish species, non-native crayfish have been introduced. The new crayfish do the same work as the original species in the ecosystem—and they can be eaten, so people who caught and sold the native crayfish now have their jobs back too.

Non-native invasive species sometimes actually help native species that are threatened with extinction. In wetlands of the southwestern United States, the native willows, cottonwoods and other plants have been replaced by tamarisk, or salt cedar. Brought to North America in the 1800s for gardens, the pretty pink shrub has now spread throughout the United States and

Some kookaburras seem to have become immune to cane toads' poison.
CAPSTOC/GETTYIMAGES

The banks of the Colorado River, once lined with native willows and cottonwood, are now clogged with tamarisk.
MISSING35MM/GETTY IMAGES

The endangered southwestern willow flycatcher now nests in invasive tamarisk and could go extinct if the tamarisk is removed.

Eco-Fact

The lands beside railways, roads and fields are often badly damaged, and few species can survive in them. Those that do are often non-native invasive species— and they do important work, such as feeding pollinators, preventing erosion and improving the soil.

The non-native African tulip tree has helped Puerto Rico's native and other species grow back, creating a lush novel ecosystem.

may soon appear in Canada. The endangered southwestern willow flycatcher traditionally nested in the native shrubs and trees but has now switched to tamarisk. If the tamarisk were removed, the willow flycatcher could go extinct.

Along with climate change and changes in the way we use land, non-native invasive species also help create *novel ecosystems*. These are *new* ecosystems that have never been seen before. Containing brand-new combinations of species, they work perfectly well, though perhaps differently from the original ecosystem. More than a third of the planet's land ecosystems are already novel ecosystems. But does the fact that they are new mean they're bad? Some ecologists believe novel ecosystems might be our best hope for the future.

THE STORY OF PUERTO RICO AND THE AFRICAN TULIP TREE

When Spanish colonists arrived in Puerto Rico in the early 1500s, they replaced most of the forest with sugarcane, coffee and tobacco plantations. Without the trees, the soil eroded and filled the rivers. Species disappeared.

When the sugar market collapsed in the 1940s, people left their farms and moved to the cities to work in factories. The forests began to return—with more than 100 non-native species that had arrived since the Spanish colonists came. These plants created shade and repaired the soil, sheltering and feeding birds and insects, which in turn helped spread seeds and pollen. The African tulip tree became the island's most common tree. But rather than crowding or shading other plants out, it allowed enough light to reach the forest floor so they could grow. Some of the native species began to come back, including plants, birds and reptiles, and today Puerto Rico's forests are novel ecosystems, consisting of both native and non-native species.

LIVING WITH CLIMATE CHANGE

The world's climate is changing—quickly. Many species will not survive the changes. But a few—considered invasive in some places—might actually thrive on things like higher temperatures and more carbon dioxide in the air. A few plants might even take more carbon dioxide out of the air and put it into the soil.

Novel ecosystems created by non-native species and climate change could continue to provide humans with the ecosystem services we depend on. Some ecologists are even trying to design new ecosystems using non-native species that can handle climate changes.

One source of inspiration is Ascension Island in the southern Atlantic Ocean. When the British **botanist** Joseph Hooker visited in 1843, the volcanic island had poor soil, no trees and little rain. Hooker thought that planting trees at the top of the island's mountain would catch moisture from the clouds, and planting trees and shrubs farther down the mountain would improve the soil. Over the next few decades, about 300 species from around the world were planted. Hooker was right.

Phragmites spread quickly in wetlands and can grow to more than 15 feet (5 meters) in height. Those same abilities make phragmites good at capturing carbon dioxide from the air, something that may help in the fight against climate change.
INVASIVE PHRAGMITES, RONDEAU, ON, AUGUST 25, 2015
JANICE GILBERT/DUCKS UNLIMITED CANADA

The bright green area in this satellite image of Ascension Island is the cloud forest created through the introduction of non-native plants in the 19th century.
JESSE ALLEN/NASA EARTH OBSERVATORY

Today the **_cloud forest_** on the island's Green Mountain is a lush tropical ecosystem.

Is this new ecosystem *better* than the original ecosystem? Maybe for humans—though not necessarily for the organisms that lived there before. However, it does show that in the face of climate change, some of the species we call non-native and invasive might turn out to be our friends.

AFRICANIZED HONEYBEES: 'KILLERS' OR FRIENDS?

In the late 1950s, a scientist in Brazil was trying to create a new strain of honeybees that would be able to cope with South American heat, like African bees, but would also be gentle, like European bees. Unfortunately the bees escaped, and Africanized honeybees, also known as "killer bees," quickly spread through South and Central America before more slowly making their way to North America.

The bees are more likely than European bees to attack anyone who nears their nests, and they will attack in much larger numbers. They're also harder for beekeepers to manage. But as European honeybees struggle with diseases, pests and pesticides, some scientists believe that the Africanized bees are better able to deal with these problems. They can also cope with the higher temperatures that climate change is bringing. So we might be very grateful for their help in pollinating our food crops if European honeybees aren't able to in the future.

European honeybees like these are less able to cope with extreme heat than Africanized bees are. So as our climate warms, unfriendly Africanized bees might become very useful to us. ED PEETERS/EYEEM/GETTYIMAGES

Removing invasive species to help restore ecosystems can be fun and satisfying work.
GREATER VICTORIA GREEN TEAM/GREENTEAMSCANADA.CA

HELPING ECOSYSTEMS REPAIR THEMSELVES

Ecological restoration helps ecosystems recover from damage caused by human activities—for example, introducing non-native species, clearing forests, damming rivers, draining swamps and using large amounts of pesticides and fertilizers. Restoration ecologists work to create the right conditions—for example, removing invasive species or reintroducing lost species or lost processes such as fire—to allow the plants, animals and other organisms to do the recovery work themselves.

The goal is to return an ecosystem *not* to the state it was in at some point in the past but to what it might have been like today if humans hadn't damaged it. (This is different from *conservation*, which aims to prevent or reduce damage to ecosystems in the first place.) With help from restoration biologists and often from lots of volunteers and others, ecosystems of all kinds—including forests, prairies, streams and wetlands—can recover some or all of the healthy diversity and balance they once had. And this in turn will help them cope with invasive species that might otherwise take over.

Ecological restoration relies on help from many volunteers—such as these two members of the Greater Victoria Green Team on southern Vancouver Island.
GREATER VICTORIA GREEN TEAM/
GREENTEAMSCANADA.CA

WHAT YOU CAN DO

While some non-native invasive species may prove helpful in a variety of ways, it's still true that they can do a lot of damage. So we need to take them seriously and do what we can to keep new non-native invasive species from taking hold, get rid of them where we can and find uses for them where we can't. Of course, much of this work is done by restoration ecologists and conservation managers, but there are lots of things you can do to help.

Find Out More

Understanding non-native invasive species and their impacts—and especially our role in the problem—is important. Learn about the non-native species that are invasive where you live so you can identify them in your neighborhood. Find out who you can tell if you think you've spotted a plant or animal that might be a problem. Governments and conservation organizations in most parts of North America have good websites on invasive species, as well as posters and booklets. And remember to keep an open mind. Some non-native invasive species might just prove helpful in the future.

Watch What You Plant

Sadly, many nurseries still sell plants that are already known to be invasive or that could become invasive. If your family has a garden, remind your parents to check online before they plant—or do it yourself. And if you're not sure, apply the precautionary principle and don't plant it at all!

Be a Good Pet Owner

If you have an aquarium, *never* dump the contents (fish, shellfish or plants) into the wild, as the organisms could take up residence there. If you're thinking of getting an exotic pet, like a snake or a lizard, do your research first. Find out what's involved in looking after it and how long it will live so you're sure you can commit to owning it. And if you have a cat, keep it inside! Cats are having huge impacts on native birds, reptiles, amphibians and small mammals around the world.

You can find lots of good information online about invasive species in your neighborhood and beyond. JOSE LUIS PELAEZ INC/GETTY IMAGES

A cat plays with the hooded warbler it has killed.
FORESTPATH/SHUTTERSTOCK.COM

INVASIVE ALL-STARS: *Cats*

The International Union for Conservation of Nature lists cats among the worst non-native invasive species. Some people argue that cats aren't really an invasive species. But whether you agree with the label or not, pet cats that are allowed to roam outdoors and *feral* cats (cats that don't belong to anyone and always live outdoors) act like an invasive species.

Cats also breed rapidly. A single female can produce up to 12 kittens per year. So their numbers have exploded— there may be as many as 80 million feral cats in the United States *plus* up to 40 million outdoor pet cats. Cats carry diseases that can harm wildlife and humans. And they kill huge numbers of birds and small mammals (not just the rodents we like them to kill). It's estimated that outdoor pet cats kill up to 4 billion birds and 22 billion mammals each year in the United States alone— and that doesn't include feral cats! Around the world, pet cats have caused the extinction of at least 63 species of birds, mammals and reptiles. Lyall's wren, a small bird on New Zealand's Stephens Island, was driven to extinction within about two years of a lighthouse keeper's arrival in 1894 with his pregnant cat, Tibbles.

So if you love cats, or if you love other animals and birds, always keep your pet cat indoors and don't feed feral cats. (Putting a bell around an outdoor cat's neck doesn't stop the killing.)

INVASIVE ALL-STARS: _Burmese Pythons_

Burmese pythons were considered cool pets in the 1980s and 1990s. The first pythons to turn up in Florida's Everglades were likely dumped there by their owners. When Hurricane Andrew hit the area in 1992, a warehouse where the snakes were being bred for pet shops was destroyed, releasing about 900 of the snakes into the Everglades. Today about 30,000 pythons lurk in Everglades National Park and the rest of southern Florida. Native mammals—raccoons, opossums, bobcats, foxes and rabbits—have all but disappeared.

The largest python ever caught in the Everglades was 17 feet (5 meters) long and 140 pounds (63 kilograms), and it contained 73 eggs. Even though they're large, the snakes are hard to catch because they're very good at hiding, especially in the Everglades' swampy terrain. They can burrow, climb trees and swim—and might have already swum from the Everglades to the Florida Keys.

Follow the Rules

If you've ever traveled to another country, you might have noticed some rules about things you can't take across the border, like certain fruits and vegetables, meats, plants, seeds and soil. It might seem like a nuisance to give up the apple that's stashed in your bag or the seeds you were hoping to plant at home, but the rules are there for a reason. The apple could be carrying an insect or other pest that could spell trouble, and the seeds could be for a plant that will be so happy where you live that it will start to spread.

In many places there are also rules about moving firewood and boats. Firewood can carry forest pests and shouldn't be moved from one area to another. Boats can carry invasive water plants and critters, with disastrous results, so they need to be carefully checked and cleaned. You might need to give parents and others a friendly reminder!

Clean Your Boots

If you and your family go for walks or hikes in different places near where you live or in places far away, make sure you clean your boots—and the rest of your clothing and gear—afterward. They might be carrying seeds of invasive plants that will drop off in the next place you go.

Volunteer

Restoration ecologists and conservation managers often rely on volunteers to help with the hard work of removing non-native invasive species. If you're interested in helping out, ask around or contact local conservation organizations. You might be able to focus on one particular place, like a park near your home, or lots of different places in your area. You'll meet other people, see neat stuff in nature and learn lots along the way.

Be a Citizen Scientist

Another great way to volunteer is by becoming a citizen scientist. Citizen scientists help gather information for scientific studies, providing scientists with data from large areas for not much cost.

The emerald ash borer, a non-native insect, was accidentally introduced in Michigan in 2002. It has since killed tens of millions of ash trees and could kill most of the 8.7 billion ash trees on this continent before it's done. Citizen scientists are doing everything from monitoring the spread of the borer to identifying ash trees that are resistant to it and observing wasps that prey on it.

Many of these programs use smartphone apps and other technologies for collecting and sending data to scientists. So participating can be a fun way to get outside and learn about technology.

Citizen scientists often get to use cool smartphone apps and other technologies to send data to scientists. FELIPE GIACOMETTI/UNSPLASH

Brushing dirt and seeds off your boots and clothing after you've been hiking can help prevent unwanted plants from moving into new areas.
CKISS—CENTRAL KOOTENAY INVASIVE SPECIES SOCIETY

Black-tailed deer are native to the west coast of North America, but human activities are causing them to function like an invasive species. EMILYNORTON/GETTY IMAGES

IN MY OWN BACKYARD

Pulling invasive plants can be hard work, but it's always fun to work with other volunteers!
GREATER VICTORIA GREEN TEAM/
GREENTEAMSCANADA.CA

Here in my garden, not far from Uplands Park, I have planted many Garry oaks, camas and other plants that are part of the local ecosystem, which helps support birds and insects. It also helps connect the remaining patches of that original ecosystem, which is good for everything that still relies on it.

But I have a new problem. It's not the English ivy, hawthorn or holly or the Himalayan blackberry that grow from seeds pooped by birds. It's not the bindweed, which is always trying to take over, or the non-native things I've planted that started spreading.

It's a native species, the black-tailed deer, and it's functioning like an invasive species. With no real predators here, since cougars and wolves stay away from cities, the deer thrive. Their numbers are growing fast. They eat my favorite plants—and farmers' crops. Ticks that live on them can give us Lyme disease. And the deer sometimes step into traffic, resulting in harm to them and to humans.

It's not their fault, of course. But I hope that one day we'll find a better balance between people and all the organisms that belong here. In the meantime, I'll tend to the native and other plants in my own garden. And I'll work with other volunteers, pulling out invasive plants in treasured places nearby. Together we'll keep the camas blooming.

Acknowledgments

First, as always, thank you, Orca, for making such beautiful books on such important topics! Special thanks to my editor, Kirstie Hudson, for spotting holes and asking the right questions, and to designer Dahlia Yuen, for making all that information bright and accessible.

My thanks to Eric Higgs, professor in the School of Environmental Studies at the University of Victoria, for reading the manuscript and setting me straight—not to mention for his own books, which have guided much of my thinking about this field over the years.

I'm also grateful to Chris Junck for his gorgeous photographs of the Garry oak meadows, to Amanda Evans of the Victoria Green Team for the photos of happy volunteers, to Mark Brown and the Monterey Middle School Ecokeepers for their hard work and their willingness to be photographed, and to Margaret Lidkea for serving as tireless leader of Friends of Uplands Park—persisting, educating and inspiring those of us who benefit in so many ways from the park. To volunteers of all ages, here and everywhere, who join in the sometimes arduous work of keeping invasive species at bay, thank you.

And, finally, to the Lekwungen Peoples on whose land we live, work and play here on the beautiful southern tip of Vancouver Island, háy̓sxʷ q̓ə!

CHRIS JUNCK

Resources

Print

Amstutz, Lisa. *Invasive Species* (from the Ecological Disasters series). Minneapolis, MN: Abdo Publishing, 2018.

Van Tol, Alex. *Aliens Among Us: Invasive Animals and Plants in British Columbia*. Victoria, BC: Royal BC Museum, 2015.

Online

Canadian Council on Invasive Species: canadainvasives.ca

Center for Invasive Species and Ecosystem Health: invasive.org

Citizen Science Portal (Government of Canada): science.gc.ca/eic/site/063.nsf/eng/h_97169.html

Eat the Invaders: eattheinvaders.org

Global Invasive Species Database: One Hundred of the World's Worst Invasive Alien Species: iucngisd.org/gisd/100_worst.php

iMapInvasives: imapinvasives.org/identification-guides

Invasive Species: *10 Species Invading North America* (Decagon TV, video, 9:21): youtube.com/watch?v=G1hJ-NmO8hE

Island Conservation: islandconservation.org/what-makes-invasive-species-damaging-islands

National Invasive Species Council (US Department of the Interior): doi.gov/invasivespecies

National Invasive Species Information Center (US Department of Agriculture): invasivespeciesinfo.gov

Plant Heroes: plantheroes.org

SciStarter: Science We Can Do Together: scistarter.org

TED Talks

The Threat of Invasive Species: Jennifer Klos, TEDEd video, March 31, 2016. 4:46: ed.ted.com/lessons/the-threat-of-invasive-species-jennifer-klos

Why Is Biodiversity So Important?: Kim Preshoff, TEDEd video, April 20, 2015. 4:19: ed.ted.com/lessons/why-is-biodiversity-so-important-kim-preshoff

Glossary

acclimatization societies—clubs formed in the 1800s for the purpose of moving plants and animals to new places

Anthropocene—a new age in which humans have changed the planet, its atmosphere and its climate

ballast water—water taken aboard a ship in one place to balance its load and then dumped in another place when the ship unloads

biodiversity—the variety and variability of living things in an ecosystem

biological control—use of one species to control another

botanist—a scientist who studies plants

capitalism—an economic system based on private ownership and profit

cells—the basic building blocks of all living things

climate change—changes in weather patterns, caused by human activity

cloud forest—a moist tropical forest immersed in cloud

Common Era—the era that began about 2,000 years ago

conservation—the science and practice of protecting and preserving ecosystems and biodiversity

conservation managers—people who work to protect species and habitats

early detection—spotting of something (like a non-native species) before it becomes a problem

ecological restoration—the science and practice of helping ecosystems recover from damage caused by human activities

ecologist—a scientist who studies ecosystems or the relationships between organisms and their environment

ecosystem—a system composed of living and nonliving things that are connected in many ways

ecosystem services—the many benefits that humans receive from healthy ecosystems

eradicate—get rid of

established—able to reproduce in a new area without human help

extinction—the total loss of a type of organism

feral—wild, not belonging to anyone

genetically modified organisms (GMOs)—plants, animals or other organisms whose genetic makeup has been altered in a laboratory, creating genetic combinations that don't occur in nature

globalization—the interdependence of people, economies and cultures driven by international trade

habitat—the place where a plant or animal normally lives

Industrial Revolution—period of economic and social change that began in England in 1760 with the shift to machine-made items and large factories

invasive species—a type of organism (usually non-native) that spreads and causes problems when it is moved (usually by humans) to a new place

native species—a type of organism that has evolved in a place without help from humans

non-native invasive species—a type of organism that people have moved to a new place, where it spreads and causes problems

non-native species—a type of organism that people have moved to a new place

novel ecosystems—ecosystems that contain new combinations of species that work perfectly well together

organism—a living thing, such as a plant, animal, insect, fish, fungus, virus or bacteria

othering—seeing or treating people or groups as alien to ourselves

pathogens—bacteria, viruses or pests that cause disease

pesticide—a chemical used to destroy pests, usually plants or animals

precautionary principle—the idea that something shouldn't be used or introduced if its effects are unknown or uncertain

predator—an organism that eats or destroys another

range—the area where an organism occurs naturally

restoration ecologists—people who work to restore damaged ecosystems

supercolony—a huge colony of ants or other organisms that is made of hundreds of smaller colonies

system—a group of things that are connected and work together in an organized way

vector—an organism that spreads other organisms to new places

weed—a plant that grows where we don't want it

xenophobia—the fear and hatred of strangers or foreigners, or of anything strange or foreign

Index

Index (continued)

MARYAM MORRISON

MERRIE-ELLEN WILCOX is a writer and editor in Victoria, British Columbia. Her first book for children, *What's the Buzz? Keeping Bees in Flight*, is part of the Orca Footprints series. When several huge Garry oak trees were cut down at the end of her street to make way for a parking lot, she became a passionate defender of the trees and the ecosystem they are part of. She studied ecological restoration at the University of Victoria and continues to naturescape her garden.